PARES SCALES

For Individual Study and Like-Instrument Class Instruction

by GABRIEL PARÈS

Revised and Edited by Harvey S. Whistler

Published for:

Flute or Piccolo . . . . Parès-Whistler

Clarinet . . . . Parès-Whistler

Oboe . . . . Parès-Whistler

Bassoon . . . . Parès-Whistler

Saxophone . . . . Parès-Whistler

Cornet, Trumpet or Baritone 𝄞 . . . . Parès-Whistler

● French Horn, Eb Alto or Mellophone . . . . Parès-Whistler

Trombone or Baritone 𝄢 . . . . Parès-Whistler

Eb Bass (Tuba - Sousaphone) . . . . Parès-Whistler

BBb Bass (Tuba - Sousaphone) . . . . Parès-Whistler

Marimba, Xylophone or Vibes . . . . Parès-Whistler-Jolliff

For Individual Study and Like-Instrument Class Instruction
(Not Playable by Bands or by Mixed-Instruments)

HAL•LEONARD CORPORATION
7777 W BLUEMOUND RD PO BOX 13819 MILWAUKEE, WI 53213

Key of C Major

Long Tones to Strengthen Lips

Scale of C

Also practice holding each tone for EIGHT counts.

When playing long tones, practice (1) ⟨ and (2) ⟨⟩.

9

10

Embouchure Studies

Slur as many tones as possible.

Slur as many tones as possible.

4

Key of F Major

Long Tones to Strengthen Lips

Also practice holding each tone for EIGHT counts.

When playing long tones practice (1) ⟍⟍ and (2) ⟍⟍⟍.

Embouchure Studies

Slur as many tones as possible.

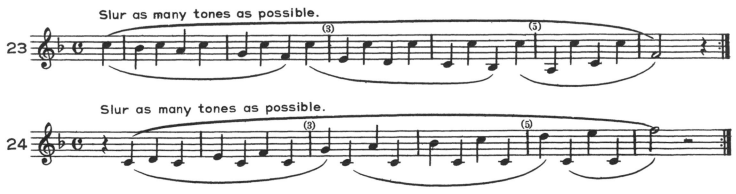

Key of G Major

Long Tones to Strengthen Lips

Also practice holding each tone for EIGHT counts.

When playing long tones, practice (1) — and (2) —.

30

31

32

Embouchure Studies

Slur as many tones as possible.

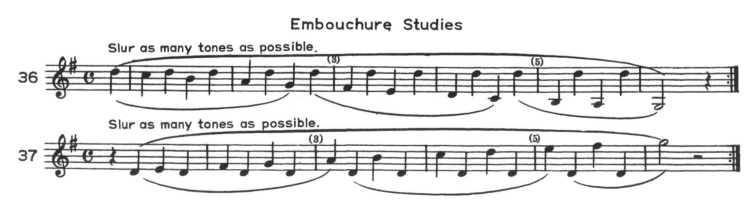

Slur as many tones as possible.

Key of B♭ Major

Long Tones to Strengthen Lips

38 Scale of B♭ (5) (9) (13)

Also practice holding each tone for EIGHT counts.

When playing long tones, practice (1) ⎯⎯◁ and (2) ▷⎯⎯◁.

39

(9) (13)

40

(5) (9)

(13)

41 (5) >

(9) >

(13) >

(17) >

42

43

44

Embouchure Studies

Slur as many tones as possible.

Slur as many tones as possible.

13

Key of D Major

Long Tones to Strengthen Lips

Also practice holding each tone for EIGHT counts.

When playing long tones, practice (1) ⎯◁ and (2) ◁▷

15

Embouchure Studies

Slur as many tones as possible.

Slur as many tones as possible.

Key of Eb Major

Long Tones to Strengthen Lips

61 Scale of Eb

Also practice holding each tone for EIGHT counts.

When playing long tones, practice (1) ⟨ and (2) ⟩

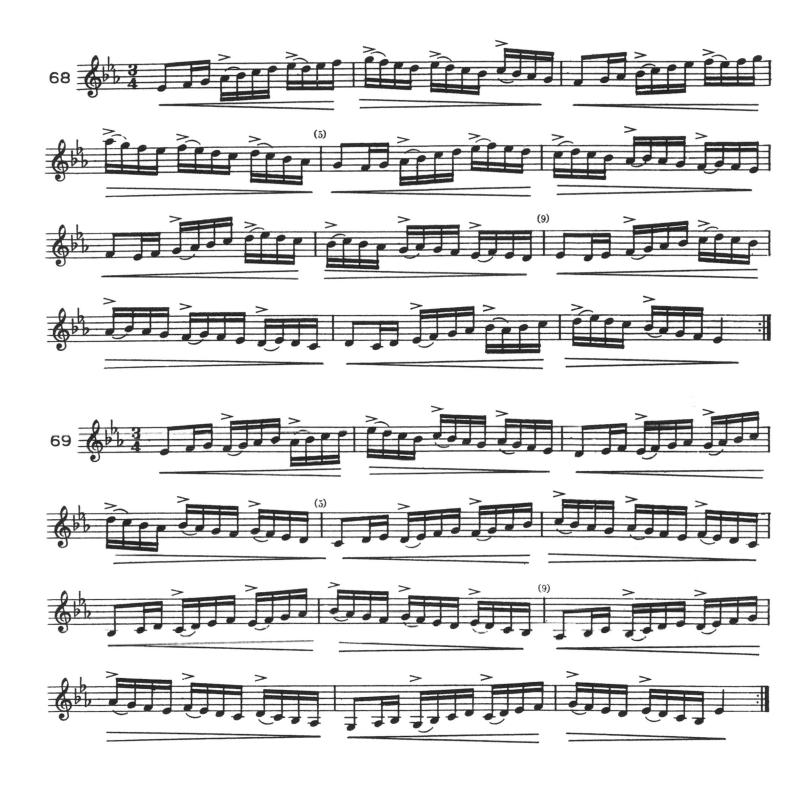

Embouchure Studies

Slur as many tones as possible.

70

Slur as many tones as possible.

71

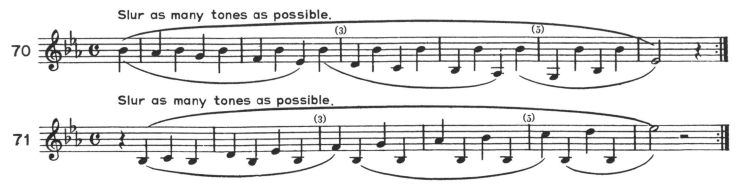

19

Key of A Major

Long Tones to Strengthen Lips

72 Scale of A

Also practice holding each tone EIGHT counts.

When playing long tones, practice (1) and (2)

73

74

75

76

77

Embouchure Studies

Slur as many tones as possible.

Slur as many tones as possible.

Key of A♭ Major

Long Tones to Strengthen Lips

Also practice holding each tone for EIGHT counts.

When playing long tones, practice (1) ◁ and (2) ◁▷.

Embouchure Studies

Slur as many tones as possible.

Key of E Major

Long Tones to Strengthen Lips

Also practice holding each tone for EIGHT counts.

When playing long tones, practice (1) ⤐ and (2) ⤐

Embouchure Studies

101

102

Slur as many tones as possible.

103

Slur as many tones as possible.

104

Key of A Minor
(Relative to the Key of C Major)

Long Tones to Strengthen Lips

Scale of A Harmonic Minor

105

Scale of A Melodic Minor

106

Also practice holding each tone for EIGHT counts.

When playing long tones, practice (1) ⟨ and (2) ⟨ ⟩

107

108

Embouchure Studies

Slur as many tones as possible.

109

Slur as many tones as possible.

110

Key of D Minor
(Relative to the Key of F Major)

Long Tones to Strengthen Lips

Scale of D Harmonic Minor

Scale of D Melodic Minor

Also practice holding each tone for EIGHT counts.

When playing long tones, practice (1) ⏤◁ and (2) ⏤◁▷.

Embouchure Studies

Slur as many tones as possible.

Slur as many tones as possible.

Key of E Minor
(Relative to the Key of G Major)

Long Tones to Strengthen Lips

Scale of E Harmonic Minor

117

Scale of E Melodic Minor

118

Also practice holding each tone for EIGHT counts.

When playing long tones, practice (1) ——◁ and (2) ◁——▷.

119

120

Embouchure Studies

Slur as many tones as possible.

121

Slur as many tones as possible.

122

Key of G Minor

(Relative to the Key of B♭ Major)

Long Tones to Strengthen Lips

Also practice holding each tone for EIGHT counts.

When playing long tones, practice (1) ———— and (2) ————

Embouchure Studies

Slur as many tones as possible.

Slur as many tones as possible.

Key of B Minor
(Relative to the Key of D Major)

Long Tones to Strengthen Lips

Also practice holding each tone for EIGHT counts.

When playing long tones, practice (1) ⟨ and (2) ⟨ ⟩

Embouchure Studies

Slur as many tones as possible.

Slur as many tones as possible.

Key of C Minor
(Relative to the Key of E♭ Major)

Long Tones to Strengthen Lips

Scale of C Harmonic Minor

Scale of C Melodic Minor

Also practice holding each tone for EIGHT counts.

When playing long tones, practice (1) ⬌ and (2) ⬌

Embouchure Studies

Slur as many tones as possible.

Slur as many tones as possible.

Key of F♯ Minor
(Relative to the Key of A Major)
Long Tones to Strengthen Lips

Scale of F♯ Harmonic Minor

141

Scale of F♯ Melodic Minor

142

Also practice holding each tone for EIGHT counts.

When playing long tones, practice (1) ——◁ and (2) ◁——▷.

143

144

Embouchure Studies

Slur as many tones as possible.

145

Slur as many tones as possible.

146

Key of F Minor

(Relative to the Key of A♭ Major)

Long Tones to Strengthen Lips

Scale of F Harmonic Minor

Scale of F Melodic Minor

Also practice holding each tone for EIGHT counts.

When playing long tones, practice (1) ⟨ and (2) ⟨ ⟩

Embouchure Studies

Slur as many tones as possible.

Slur as many tones as possible.

Key of C# Minor

(Relative to the Key of E Major)

Long Tones to Strengthen Lips

Scale of C# Harmonic Minor

Scale of C# Melodic Minor

Also practice holding each tone for EIGHT counts.

When playing long tones, practice (1) $\longrightarrow$ and (2) $\longrightarrow$

Embouchure Studies

Slur as many tones as possible.

Slur as many tones as possible.

Major Scales

Harmonic Minor Scales

Melodic Minor Scales

Arpeggios

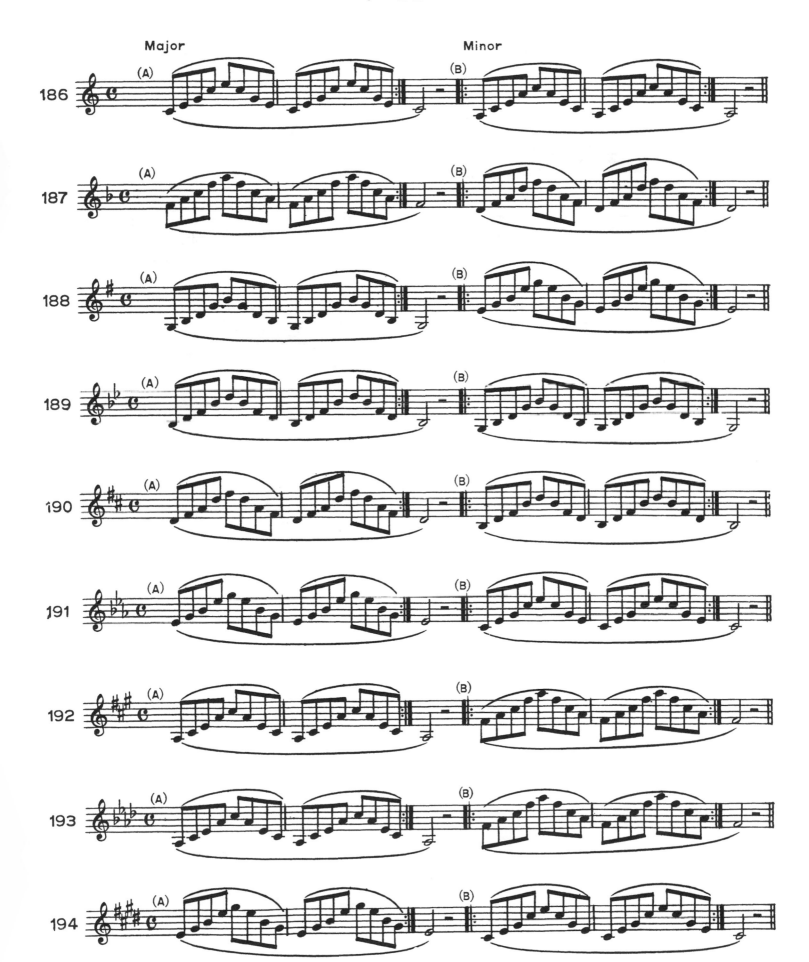

Chromatic Scales

Chromatic Scales in Triplets

Two Octave Chromatic Scales

Two Octave Chromatic Scales in Triplets

Chromatic Exercise

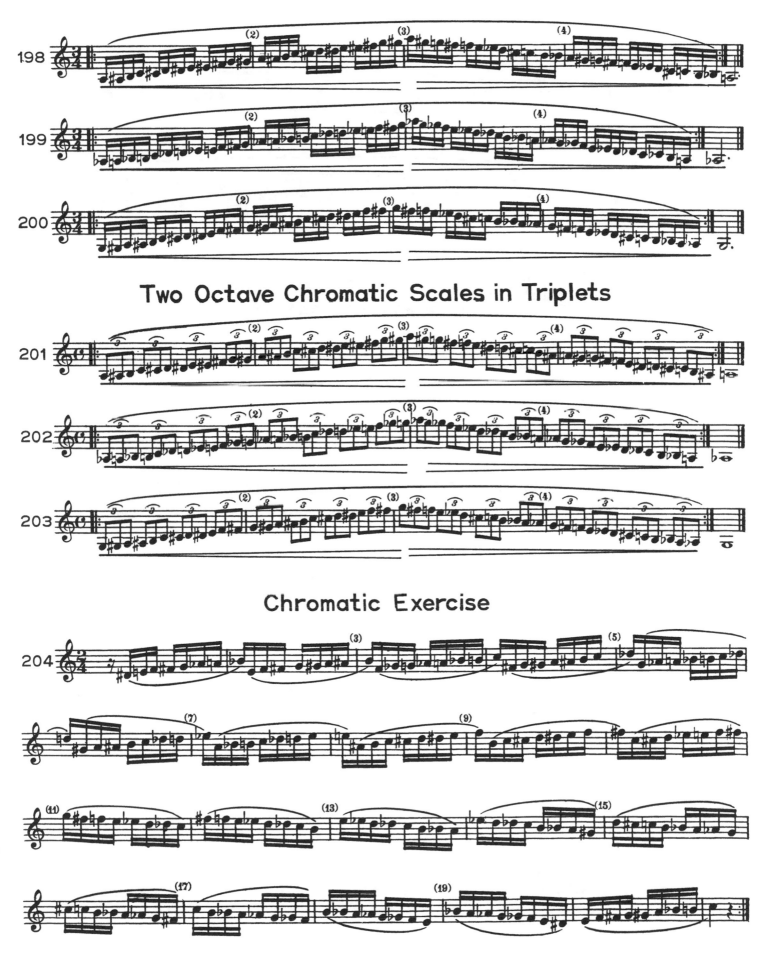

Studies in Mechanism

Interval Exercises

Slurs

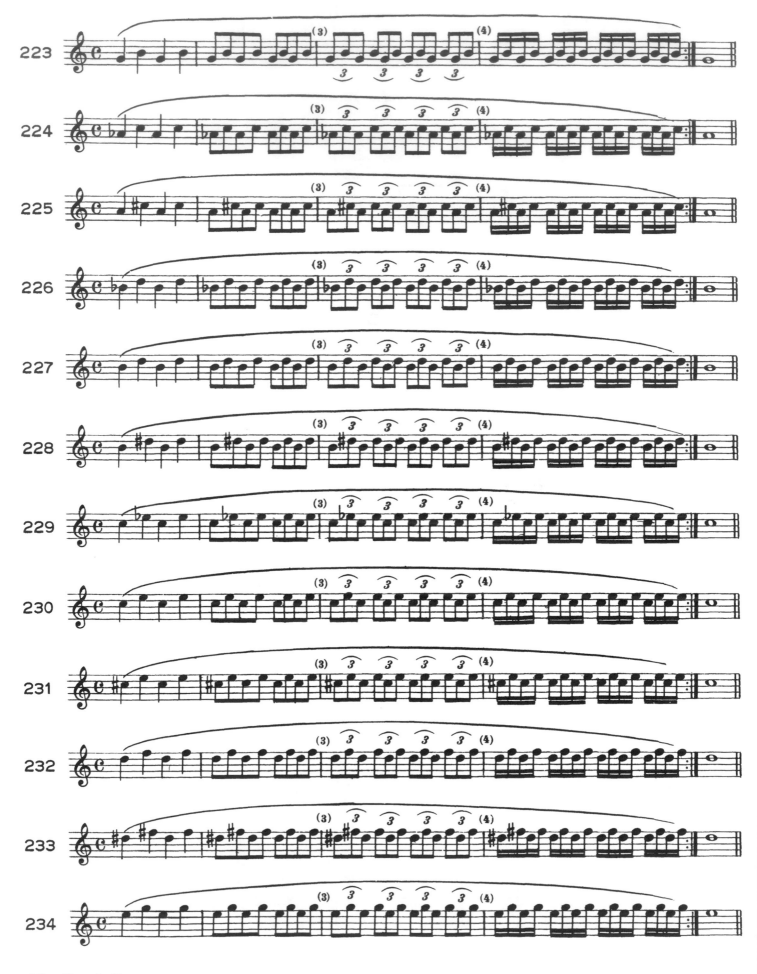

Study in Thirds

Study in Fourths

Combined Fifths and Sixths

Combined Sevenths and Octaves

Triplet Study

Octave Study

Octave Study in Triplets